N

LaNd Habitats

Introducing Habitats

Bobbie Kalman and John Crossingham

Crabtree Publishing Company

www.crabtreebooks.com

Created by Bobbie Kalman

Dedicated by Louise Mayer
To Cedric Lukan Busch, may you always see the world with the same sense of wonder;
eyes wide with amazement. Love ya!

Editor-in-Chief
Bobbie Kalman

Writing team
Bobbie Kalman
John Crossingham

Substantive editor
Kelley MacAulay

Editors
Molly Aloian
Michael Hodge
Kathryn Smithyman

Design
Katherine Kantor
Margaret Amy Salter (cover)
Samantha Crabtree (series logo)

Production coordinator
Heather Fitzpatrick

Photo research
Crystal Foxton

Special thanks to
Jack Pickett and Karen Van Atte

Illustrations
Barbara Bedell: pages 9, 17, 18, 32 (bottom left)
Katherine Kantor: pages 22, 25
Bonna Rouse: pages 10, 16, 19, 32 (top right)
Tiffany Wybouw: page 32 (top left)

Photographs
© De La Harpe, Roger / Animals Animals - Earth Scenes: page 18
Visuals Unlimited: Albert J. Copley: page 17
Other images by Corel, Creatas, Digital Stock, Digital Vision, and Photodisc

Library and Archives Canada Cataloguing in Publication
Kalman, Bobbie, date.
   Land habitats / Bobbie Kalman & John Crossingham.

(Introducing habitats)
ISBN-13: 978-0-7787-2948-8 (bound)
ISBN-13: 978-0-7787-2976-1 (pbk.)
ISBN-10: 0-7787-2948-6 (bound)
ISBN-10: 0-7787-2976-1 (pbk.)

   1. Habitat (Ecology)--Juvenile literature. I. Crossingham, John, date.
II. Title. III. Series.

QH541.14.K3425 2006   j577   C2006-904508-9

Library of Congress Cataloging-in-Publication Data
Kalman, Bobbie.
   Land habitats / Bobbie Kalman & John Crossingham.
     p. cm. -- (Introducing habitats)
   ISBN-13: 978-0-7787-2948-8 (rlb)
   ISBN-10: 0-7787-2948-6 (rlb)
   ISBN-13: 978-0-7787-2976-1 (pb)
   ISBN-10: 0-7787-2976-1 (pb)
   1. Habitat (Ecology)--Juvenile literature. I. Crossingham, John, date.
II. Title. III. Series.

QH541.14.K34965 2007
577--dc22

2006024905

Crabtree Publishing Company

www.crabtreebooks.com   1-800-387-7650

Published in Canada
Crabtree Publishing
616 Welland Ave.
St. Catharines, ON
L2M 5V6

Published in the United States
Crabtree Publishing
PMB16A
350 Fifth Ave., Suite 3308
New York, NY 10118

Published in the United Kingdom
Crabtree Publishing
White Cross Mills
High Town, Lancaster
LA1 4XS

Published in Australia
Crabtree Publishing
386 Mt. Alexander Rd.
Ascot Vale (Melbourne)
VIC 3032

Contents

Land habitats

A **habitat** is a place in nature.
Plants grow in habitats. Animals
live in habitats. Many animals
make homes in their habitats.

Living in land habitats

Many plants and animals live in land habitats. Land habitats are not all the same. **Forests** are land habitats that have a lot of trees. **Deserts** are land habitats that do not have a lot of trees. Deserts are sandy and rocky.

Everything they need

There are **living things** in land habitats.
Plants and animals are living things. There
are also **non-living things** in land habitats.
Rocks and dirt are non-living things.

Staying alive

Plants and animals need food, air, and water to stay alive. Plants and animals find everything they need to stay alive in their habitats. This gorilla found food in its habitat.

Rainforest habitats

Forests are areas of land that are covered with trees. Some forests are **rain forests**. Rain forests are in parts of the world where a lot of rain falls. Rain helps plants grow. Many plants grow in rain forests. They grow close together.

Living in the forest

Some rainforest animals live mainly in trees. Birds, snakes, and ring-tailed lemurs live mainly in trees. Other rainforest animals live on the ground. The ground in a rain forest is called the **forest floor**. Mountain lions and lizards live on the forest floor.

Ring-tailed lemurs live in trees.

9

Colors and calls

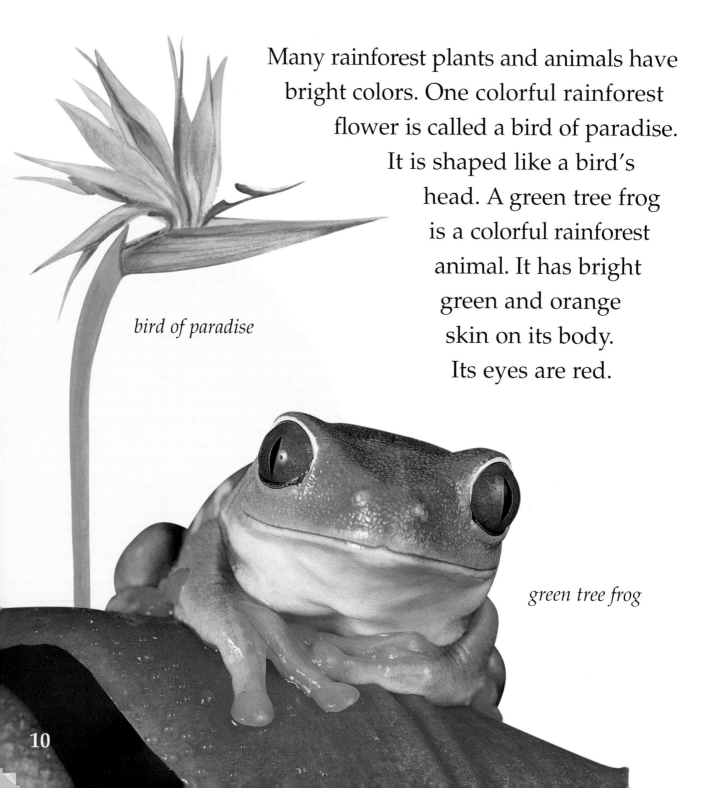

Many rainforest plants and animals have bright colors. One colorful rainforest flower is called a bird of paradise. It is shaped like a bird's head. A green tree frog is a colorful rainforest animal. It has bright green and orange skin on its body. Its eyes are red.

bird of paradise

green tree frog

10

Shout it out!

Rain forests can be noisy places! Some rainforest birds make **calls**. Calls are loud noises. These rainbow lorikeets make loud calls. Monkeys make screeching and hooting sounds.

Mountain habitats

Mountains are tall, steep areas of land. They are much taller than hills. At the top of tall mountains, the weather is windy and cold all year. The tops of mountains are snowy and rocky. There are few plants. Trees do not grow high up on mountains.

Mountain forests

At the bottom of some mountains, the weather is warm and rainy. Forests grow at the bottom of most mountains. Many animals live in the forests. This giant panda lives in a mountain forest.

Life on top

Only certain animals live at the top of mountains. Mountain top habitats are cold. Snow leopards and mountain goats live high up on mountains. These animals have thick fur. Their fur keeps them warm.

Steep slopes

Few animals can walk on the side of steep, rocky mountains. Mountain goats have tough coverings on their feet. The coverings are called **hooves**. Hooves protect a mountain goat's feet. A mountain goat can run on steep rocks without hurting its feet.

Cool caves

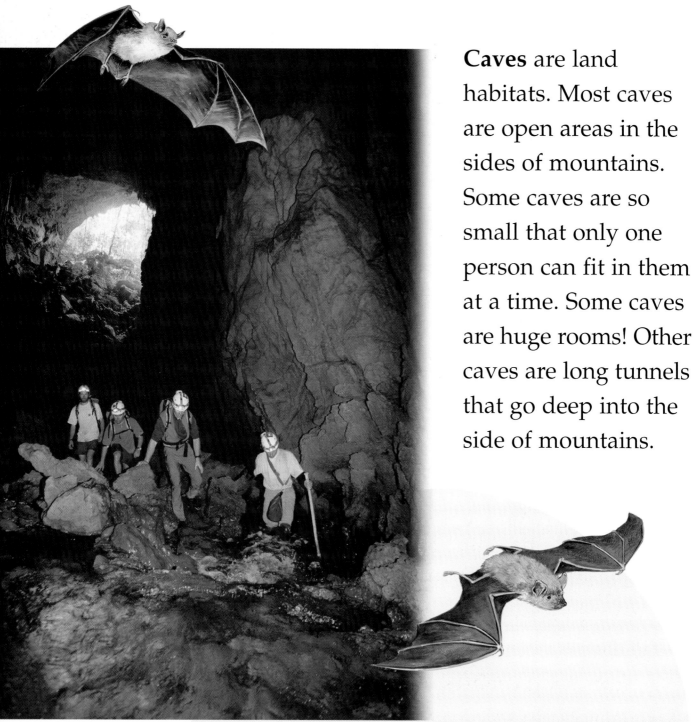

Caves are land habitats. Most caves are open areas in the sides of mountains. Some caves are so small that only one person can fit in them at a time. Some caves are huge rooms! Other caves are long tunnels that go deep into the side of mountains.

No sunshine

Caves are dark habitats. The sun does
not shine into caves. Most caves are cold
because they are not heated by the sun.
Many caves are also damp. Water drips
down from their ceilings. There are
pools of water in some caves.

Cave life

Caves are habitats for some plants and animals. Mosses are plants that grow in caves. Mosses can grow in dark places. Animals called bats live in caves. Bats live in groups. A group of bats is called a **colony**. Thousands of bats often live together in one colony! A large colony of bats needs to live in a large cave.

moss on a rock

Sleeping in

Caves are winter habitats for some bears.
In winter, it is warmer inside a cave than it
is outside the cave. Bears sleep in their caves
for a long time. Sometimes they wake up to
look for food. When the weather becomes
warm in spring, the bears leave the cave.

Grassland habitats

There are **grassland** habitats in many parts of the world. Grasslands are flat areas of land. They are covered with grasses. There are also bushes and wildflowers in grasslands. Grasslands have very few trees.

Eating grassland plants

Many grassland animals eat plants. Animals that eat plants are called **herbivores**. Different grassland herbivores eat different plants. Many grassland herbivores eat grasses. Other herbivores eat bushes and parts of trees. This mother kangaroo is eating grass.

Grassland groups

Many grassland animals live in groups.
Prairie dogs are grassland animals that
live in groups. Prairie dogs live under
the ground. They dig large homes called
towns. Towns are made up of long tunnels.

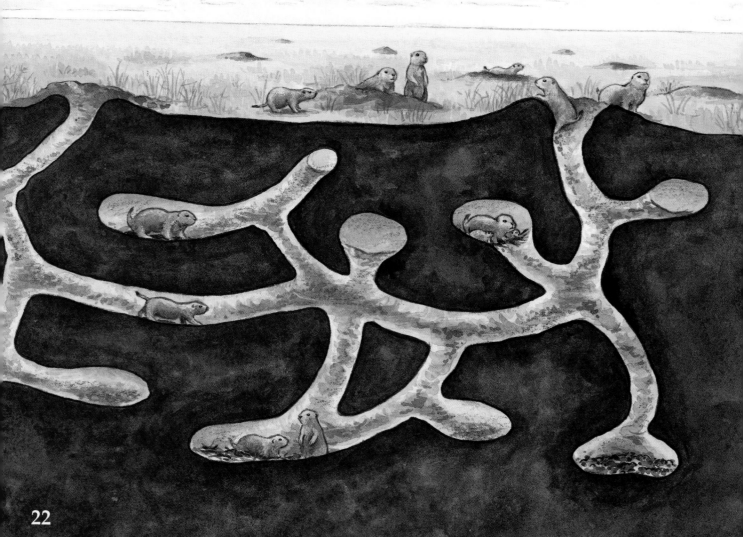

Groups above the ground

Some grassland animals live in groups above the ground. Zebras live in groups. Groups of zebras are called **herds**. Herds of zebras travel from place to place to find food and water.

Desert habitats

Deserts are hot, dry land habitats. Deserts are dry because they get very little rain. There is not enough water in deserts for most plants to stay alive. Cacti are plants that do not need much water. Most desert plants are cacti.

Finding water

When it rains in the desert, cacti take in water. They store the water in their stems. Desert animals also need water to stay alive. Some animals can get the water they need by eating parts of cacti. When the animals eat the plants, they get some of the water that is stored in the cacti. This iguana is eating part of a cactus plant.

Some cacti are small and round. Other cacti are tall and thin.

Keeping cool

Many animals live in deserts. Bats, lizards, jack rabbits, and kit foxes live in deserts. Animals need to keep cool in hot deserts. Some animals keep cool by resting in the shade. These kit foxes are resting in the shade.

Active at night

Deserts are cooler at night than they are during the day. Many desert animals search for food at night when the weather is cool. They sleep during the day. This scorpion hunts at night.

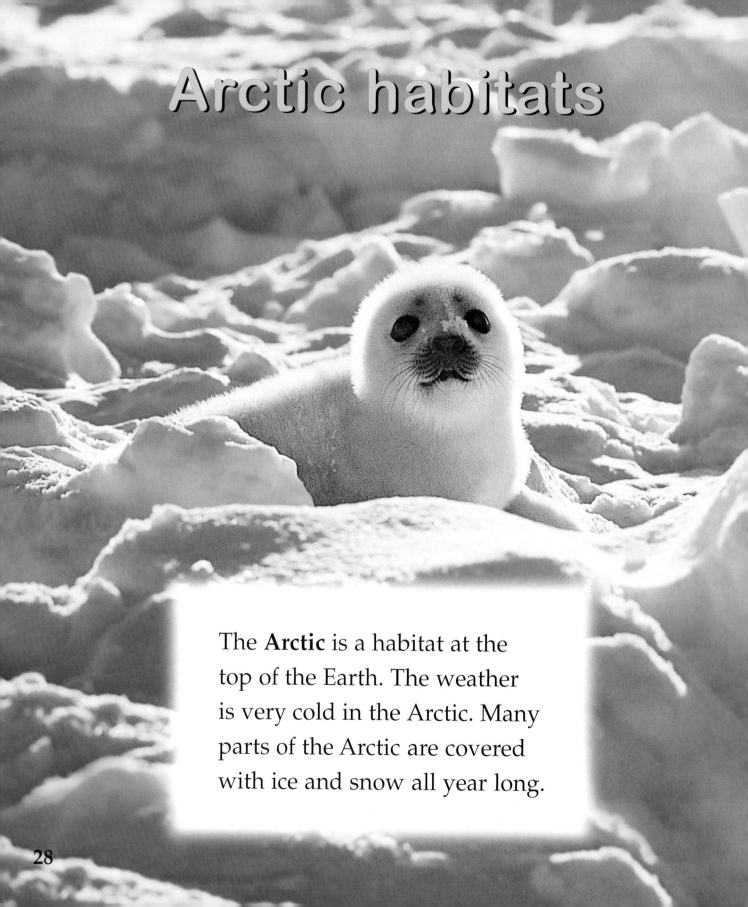

Arctic habitats

The **Arctic** is a habitat at the
top of the Earth. The weather
is very cold in the Arctic. Many
parts of the Arctic are covered
with ice and snow all year long.

Long winter, short summer

Winter lasts nearly all year in the Arctic. The weather in winter is freezing! Summer lasts only a few weeks. Even in summer, the Arctic does not get very warm. The snow melts only in some places. This polar bear is resting on some grass in summer.

Arctic animals

Arctic hares, arctic foxes, and lemmings are animals that live in the Arctic. Many arctic animals are **carnivores**. Carnivores are animals that eat other animals. Many Arctic animals are carnivores because there are few plants in the Arctic. This arctic fox is catching a mouse to eat.

Big paws

Some arctic animals have big paws.
Having big paws helps keep the animals
from sinking into the snow. Polar bears
have four big, wide paws. This arctic
hare has two big back paws. It uses
its big paws to run on top of the snow.

Words to know and Index

animals
pages 4, 5, 6, 7, 9, 10,
13, 14, 15, 18, 21, 22,
23, 25, 26, 27, 30, 31

Arctic
pages 28-31

caves
pages 16-19

deserts
pages 5, 24-27

grasslands
pages 20-23

mountains
pages 12-15, 16

plants
pages 4, 5, 6, 7, 8, 10,
12, 18, 21, 24, 25, 30

rain forests
pages 8-11

Other index words
big paws 31
carnivores 30
habitats 4, 5, 6, 7, 14, 16,
17, 18, 19, 20, 24, 28
herbivores 21
herds 23
keeping cool 26-27
warm fur 14